# FACING DOWN OUR FEARS

## Finding Courage When Anxiety Grips the Heart

## Adult Journal

Dedicated to Donna Carlisle, who served the Chapel faithfully and during the hard times always said, "We're going to make it!"

## Contents

*This journal was created with input from more than 30 pastors and laypersons from across North America.*

Writing team: David R. Mains, Director; Dennis Clements, France French, Patric Knaak, Marian Oliver, Randy Petersen, Mitchell Vander Vorst.

Editor: Marian Oliver
Editorial Coordinator: Mitchell Vander Vorst
Cover Design: Scott Rattray
Cover Illustration: Marilyn King
Text Design: Blum Graphic Design

ISBN 1-879050-47-1

# INTRODUCTION

**W**e used to be afraid of nuclear bombs. Now we fear terrorists, earthquakes, and crime in the streets. It's always something.

Apart from those external dangers, many of us have deep inner fears. What will people think of me? Will I measure up? What if I try something and fail miserably?

Parents fear for their children. Will they turn out all right? Will there be any kind of a world left for them? And as adult children watch their parents grow older, many fear the ravages of the aging process.

What a rosy picture we have painted here! But God's message comes clear to a world that cowers in terror: "Fear not!" If God's "got the whole world in his hands," why should his children be afraid? Our trust in God should set us apart from our fretful neighbors. In the bleakest of circumstances, we have a bright hope (which may make people wonder about us sometimes). Imagine the effect a confident, hopeful church could have in this world! "For God did not give us a spirit of timidity, but a spirit of power, of love and of self-discipline" (2 Timothy 1:7).

That's what this 50-Day Spiritual Adventure is about—tossing out our timidity and developing the love, power, and self-discipline we need in a world that seems to be getting out of hand. Scripture, prayer, and some fun activities will keep us focused on the Lord of life.

A little boy came running home one day in tears and fears after a run-in with the school bully. But the next day he walked up to the bully, looked him in the eye, and said, "I'm not afraid of you!" What made the difference? His father was standing behind him.

With a loving and powerful Father standing behind us, we can face down any fear. During this Adventure, we'll focus on eight fears we need to face down.

---

**Week 1:** Face down the fear of a society that's breaking down.

**Week 2:** Face down the fear of living insignificant lives.

**Week 3:** Face down the fear of rejection.

**Week 4:** Face down the fear of the big "F" (failure).

**Week 5:** Face down the unhealthy fear of God.

**Week 6:** Face down the fear of sickness, aging, and death.

**Week 7:** Face down the fear of threats to our children.

**Week 8:** Face down the fear of the rise of evil.

# HOW TO USE THIS JOURNAL

**S**everal hundred thousand people across North America will join you in this Spiritual Adventure. Like you, they'll set aside 50 days to focus on finding courage in Christ to face down fears. This unique study should prove to be a time of refreshment, renewal, and accelerated growth for individuals and churches alike. The Adventure involves five spiritual disciplines, including Scripture reading and prayer, that you'll be doing throughout the 50 days. By incorporating these disciplines into your daily routine, you will develop godly habits as you trust the Holy Spirit to work in your life.

One of the disciplines is to study Scripture daily and memorize five short passages during the Adventure. Another discipline involves praying a simple prayer each day. We've provided a sample for you to use as a guide. The remaining three disciplines, with the two mentioned above, are explained in detail on pages 6–12.

Once you've familiarized yourself with the five disciplines, all you need to do to complete this Adventure is follow the journal each day. In addition to the Scripture readings and questions, you'll find reminders to help you keep up with the other disciplines. Journal-keeping is a good way to measure your progress. You may want to look back in a couple of weeks and remind yourself of the ways you've grown in facing down fears.

We suggest setting aside 15 to 20 minutes a day for this Adventure. (Of course, you can meditate on the chosen Scripture passages and questions for as long as you like.) Some of the disciplines will take a little extra effort, but they will come up only a few times during the 50 days. If you plan on using the Adventure together as a family or with one or more

### How *Not* to Do the Adventure

**"The New Testament on cassette helped some but ever since I got this 'Prayer On Tape' series my devotional life has really taken off!"**

friends, you will probably need to allow more time. On pages 71–74 you'll find suggestions on how to set aside a special Adventure time. We are sure that the benefits will be well worth your investment.

Experts claim that it takes about 21 days to form a habit—good or bad. So this 50-Day Adventure should give you ample time to establish spiritual habits that will continue beyond Day 50. And if after 50 days you're looking for a way to keep some of the disciplines going, we have a suggestion on page 76.

It may help you to keep track of everything by filling in the date in the space provided for each day. If you fall behind don't give up or get discouraged. You don't need to go over what you missed. Just get back on track with the current day's assignment. God is always ready to give you a fresh start and strengthen you as you press on in your journey.

The Adventure is easier and more exciting when you team up with someone else. Being accountable is a good way to make sure you get the most out of these 50 days. Consider joining with a fellow believer or group of believers, and encourage one another along the way. If your church is doing the study, ask a fellow adventurer to pray for you and check on your progress regularly. Offer to do the same for him or her.

Another source of encouragement will be *The Chapel of the Air* radio broadcasts, heard Monday through Saturday, and the *You Need to Know* television program, aired Monday through Friday. These special Adventure programs will feature the themes and Scripture readings for each day. To find out when these programs are aired in your area, call your local Christian radio/TV station or write to The Chapel Ministries, Box 30, Wheaton, IL 60189, (708)690-2800.

For additional insights on the eight Adventure topics, you may wish to read *Scared to Life* by Douglas Rumford. Contact your church, your local Christian bookstore, or The Chapel of the Air Ministries (see p. 14). We have also made suggestions throughout the journal of additional resources to help you relate to specific fears we need to face down.

### Take a few minutes now to prepare for the Adventure.

Start by familiarizing yourself with the five disciplines. Read pages 6–12. It will also be helpful to flip through the day-to-day pages of the journal starting on page 17. This way you will have an idea of what will be coming. Then on the Friday before Day 1 of the Adventure, begin the Warm-up Day exercises (p. 15) to give you a head start.

## Face the Unknown with Confidence in the Known

Whenever you feel afraid . . . just whistle a happy tune. That was the musical advice to a young boy in the Broadway show *The King and I*. You can't control the fearful things that may happen around you, but you can focus on something bright, cheerful, and musical.

The psalmist had a more profound idea in mind when he prayed, "Even though I walk through the valley of the shadow of death, I will fear no evil, for you are with me" (Psalm 23:4). Even in the most frightening circumstances, he could focus on the presence of his powerful Lord.

What shadowy valleys are you walking through these days? Are you afraid of the future, the unknown, some disaster that may befall you, or even death? Are you worried about what will become of our society? Perhaps you fear failure, criticism, or that your life will be insignificant.

In the face of such fears, as a Christian, you can "whistle a happy tune," and the psalmist tells us how that tune goes: "You are with me." Christ is with us as we face our fears, and he offers us great comfort. Where do we find his words of comfort and strength? In the Bible, of course. So why not store his words in our heart—and in our memory? Study them, learn them, meditate on them, recite them, even sing them. Then when you're afraid of the unknown, you can focus on the Known and his words of reassurance.

**Assignment:** Each day of the Adventure, study the assigned Scripture passage and answer the questions in the journal. (Note that Saturday and Sunday are usually combined.) During the 50 days you'll be asked also to memorize verses. We've selected eight Scripture passages, from which you can choose at least five to learn. In-depth study questions on these scriptures appear in the journal on the weekends. Go over the verses repeatedly, committing them to memory. You'll have an opportunity to use them daily as part of the prayer discipline in this Adventure (Discipline 2). For added help, consider obtaining a Scripture memory pack tailor-made for this series. (See the order form on p. 78.)

Hint: It might be easier if you can work with someone else to learn the Scripture memory passages. Find a friend or family member to encourage you and check your progress. If your whole family is doing this Adventure, your children also will be memorizing verses. They may be even better at it than you are! Be learners together.

## Scripture Memory Passage
## Suggestions for Adults:

*Choose five of the eight passages listed below to memorize.*

Chosen          Memorized

**Week 1:**     *The Fear of a Society That's Breaking Down*
☐               ☐     John 16:33

**Week 2:**     *The Fear of Living Insignificant Lives*
☐               ☐     Romans 8:15–16

**Week 3:**     *The Fear of Rejection*
☐               ☐     Hebrews 13:6

**Week 4:**     *The Fear of the Big "F" (Failure)*
☐               ☐     Psalm 37:23–24

**Week 5:**     *The Unhealthy Fear of God*
☐               ☐     Psalm 103:13

**Week 6:**     *The Fear of Sickness, Aging, and Death*
☐               ☐     Psalm 23:4

**Week 7:**     *The Fear of Threats to Our Children*
☐               ☐     Psalm 103:17

**Week 8:**     *The Fear of the Rise of Evil*
☐               ☐     2 Thessalonians 3:3

*Check the first box when you choose to memorize the scripture.*
*Check the second box when you have memorized it.*

## Personalize the "Facing Down Our Fears Prayer"

A fire breaks out. Or there's an accident and someone's been hurt. Perhaps a crime is being committed. In such terrifying situations, there's something that millions of North Americans can do to make things better. They call 9-1-1.

These people don't know how to fight fires or crime. But they do know who to call. Soon the trained experts will be on their way. They will take care of things. The call to 9-1-1 does not totally erase our fears, but it soothes them. We have done what we could.

In today's world, many fear that society is disintegrating. We find violence in the streets, broken families, declining morals. In their own way, these issues are as frightening—if not more frightening—as any accident or emergency. But Christians need not be overcome by such fears. We can make our "9-1-1" call, not to an emergency operator but to God himself. We can put the situation in his hands and trust in his expertise.

We're not running away from the problems of our world, we're calling on the One who can help. We refuse to be tormented by fear. Instead, we determine to live lives of significance even in difficult times. God's got the whole world in his hands, he knows what to do, and he has roles for each of us to play in helping his kingdom grow.

**Assignment:** Daily during the Adventure, pray the Facing Down Our Fears Prayer. Use the following model, but make the words your own. You'll note that there are two blanks to fill in as you pray each day: a situation where you're not at peace, and a memory verse you've learned. There is tremendous power in naming a specific fear or concern and then facing it down with God's Word.

---

*Facing Down Our Fears Prayer*

*Lord, I know that when I feel afraid, you want to calm my heart. Yet at this moment, I'm not at peace about _____.*
*The enemy wants me to be consumed by this fear.*
*But your Word reminds me:*

[FILL IN MEMORY VERSE].

*Thank you that as I face down my fears, you are always with me. Amen.*

---

## Encourage Others by Being a Barnabas

The man had been a terrorist, hunting down members of the enemy group and kidnapping them. Suddenly, he had a change of heart and switched sides. Now he claimed to be part of the group that he used to terrorize. He wanted to meet with the group's leaders, but they were still afraid of him. Perhaps it was all a trick.

The early Christians knew this terrorist as Saul, persecutor of the church, but we know him as Paul, God's messenger to the Gentiles. If it weren't for Barnabas, Paul might never have become an apostle. It was Barnabas who took a chance on this former enemy, and brought him as a friend to the other Christian leaders (Acts 9). Later, when Paul rejected young John Mark for a missionary trip because Mark had left him on their first journey, it was Barnabas who stood up for Mark. The very name Barnabas means "Son of Encouragement"—and that is what he was.

All of us need a Barnabas once in a while, someone to come alongside us when we feel discouraged or fearful. And each of us is called to be a Barnabas. "Encourage one another," says the Book of Hebrews.

Yet some of us shy away from reaching out to others because we're afraid of what they will think. We fear that we will be rejected. Some of us have experienced painful rejection, and we don't want to go through that again. So we play it safe. We keep others at arm's length because, if we really knew each other, the friendship might fail.

The best way to face down rejection is to practice showing acceptance, as Barnabas did so well. Some people may reject us, but God accepts us, so we can accept others. As we reach out in true friendship, we can actually reject the spirit of rejection. "You may keep me out of your club,"

**Though she hadn't read it yet, Lois had a
strong sense of foreboding about her annual review.**

we say to those who reject us, "but I won't let that bother me. I'll start my own club where all are welcome." It is the way of Christ, who freely welcomes us by his grace. It is the way of Barnabas, the encourager.

**Assignment:** Look around your church, your workplace, your neighborhood, for someone who may need the encouragement of a Barnabas. Think about times in your own life when you've needed some extra support. Perhaps your experience will give you compassion for someone in a similar situation now. As names come to mind, write them below, both now and during the 50 days.

Three times during the Adventure, be a Barnabas to someone. Make them feel like an insider. Show that you think they're important by making a phone call, sending a card, offering to pray for them, and so on. A creative idea from the heart can turn a recipient's bad day into a good one. As you take the risk to encourage others, you'll not only show them acceptance, but you'll be facing down your own fears of rejection.

As you choose people to encourage put a check in the first box by their name. When you have been an encourager for someone, check the second box.

☐ 1     ☐ 2     _____

☐ 1     ☐ 2     _____

☐ 1     ☐ 2     _____

☐ 1     ☐ 2     _____

☐ 1     ☐ 2     _____

☐ 1     ☐ 2     _____

## Dare to Pull Off an Outrageously Courageous Act

In the spring of 1994, one of the best basketball players in history decided to play baseball. When Michael Jordan first announced his intentions, most sports fans laughed or scratched their heads. What would make this popular athlete take a chance like this? Jordan just said he was not afraid of failure.

The fear of failure has paralyzed many. People refuse to try new things because they think they might fail. They assume they will become laughingstocks, targets of mockery for everyone around them. Better to stay safe and avoid risks.

But that's not God's way. Scripture is packed with risk-takers. People of faith tend to go boldly where no one has gone before. You may recall from Jesus' parable that the servant with one talent was scolded for not taking a chance with it. He was afraid that the master would be angry if he lost it. Instead, the master wanted him to risk it (Matthew 25:14–30).

Is there a "talent" that you've buried in the ground? Why not take a chance and use it? Is there something you've always wanted to do, but you've been afraid to try? Why not "go for it" in this Adventure? Stare the possibility of failure full in the face, and laugh at it by attempting some outrageously courageous act. By *outrageously courageous*, we mean something that is beyond the boundaries of what would normally seem reasonable to you. Hey, you may fail. But you can learn from that. Just pick yourself up, dust yourself off, and try again.

Don't let the fear of failure keep you from finding a new way to glorify God.

**Assignment:** Once during this Adventure, do an outrageously courageous act on behalf of the Lord—something you wouldn't normally dare to do. An outrageously courageous act for you might be talking to a friend about Christ, or just getting to know the person next door. Maybe it's volunteering to tutor in the inner city or counselling women facing unplanned pregnancies. Maybe it's using a hidden talent in church—singing a solo or teaching a class or (gulp!) tending the nursery. Whatever, give it a try.

Use the questions on page 41 to help you prepare for your outrageously courageous act by naming your fears and analyzing them, and by seeking God's guidance and strength. Afterwards, evaluate your effort (also on p. 41).

## Break Free from the Unhealthy Fear of God

Kittens are frustrating. They're so cuddly, you want to hold them and pet them. But when you step toward them to pick them up, they scamper away. They are, quite literally, "scaredy cats." You intend to show them love, but you're so much bigger than they are, they fear your power.

Sometimes we're like that with God. He longs to show us love, but we respond in fear. He wants to forgive our sins and welcome us into his arms, but we scamper away in guilt and terror.

But isn't the fear of the Lord "the beginning of wisdom," as it says in Proverbs? Absolutely. God's way begins with the understanding that he is God. He's bigger and stronger than we are, and we must answer to him. But Scripture doesn't stop there, and neither should we. The New Testament reports on God's amazing love. It says, "Perfect love drives out fear" (1 John 4:18).

Yet too many Christians see God as an unapproachable judge, frowning in disapproval over each detail of their lives. Such people can be guilt-ridden and may tend to judge others.

The Bible shows us a God who is understanding and loving, a God who laughs and surprises us, a God who not only loves us but *likes us* and wants to spend time with us. Righteous and holy? Yes! But he's helping us, step by step, to be righteous and holy, too.

**Assignment:** During the first four weeks of the Adventure, read two chapters each week of the small book *How to Fear God Without Being Afraid of Him*. This fast-moving book by David New and Randy Petersen has been created specifically for this Adventure. To obtain your copy, see page 52. This book is also available on tape.

After you've completed the book, consider this fun idea to help you process what you've discovered about God and your relationship with him. Schedule a special meal with family or friends to talk about what you've learned through the book. This gathering could also serve as a kind of mid-Adventure checkup. Think of a place you enjoy, where you could sit and talk for a while. A delightful time for you might be taking your family out for breakfast at a local restaurant, or inviting friends over for a Saturday night dessert. Pick the ideal setting, and begin planning for it.

The daily questions in the journal during Week 5 and the questions in *How to Fear God Without Being Afraid of Him* might help your discussion. If you make this a family time, you may be able to use some of the ideas on pages 71–74. Pray that through this gathering God will draw you closer to him and those you love.

# SUMMARY OF DISCIPLINE ASSIGNMENTS

Read this summary to get acquainted with the Adventure and to see how often the various discipline assignments are to be done. (For a full description of the disciplines, see pp. 6–12.) Remember: This journal will give you daily reminders to guide you through the assignments.

**Daily**    Discipline 1:
### Face the Unknown with Confidence in the Known

Study the assigned Scripture passages and answer the questions in the journal each day.

Choose five short memory passages from the eight listed on page 7. Work throughout the Adventure to store these words in your heart.

Discipline 2:
### Personalize the "Facing Down Our Fears Prayer"

Pray the Facing Down Our Fears Prayer, using the model on page 8.

**Weekly**    Discipline 5:
### Break Free from the Unhealthy Fear of God

Weeks 1–4: Read two chapters each week in *How to Fear God Without Being Afraid of Him*. Then, before the Adventure is over, plan a special meal with family or friends where you can discuss what you've learned through the book.

**Three Times During the Adventure**

Discipline 3:
### Encourage Others by Being a Barnabas

Look for people you may be able to encourage. Three times during the Adventure, show support to someone through a kind deed or word.

**Once During the Adventure**

Discipline 4:
### Dare to Pull Off an Outrageously Courageous Act

Seeking God's guidance and strength, do something courageous on behalf of the Lord—something you normally wouldn't dare to do. Use the questions on page 41 to help you prepare for and evaluate your effort.

# Make Your Adventure the Best It Can Be!

*Here are two wonderful suggestions for enhancing your Adventure experience.*

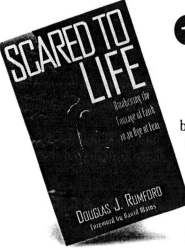

**1** Read *Scared to Life: Awakening the Courage of Faith in an Age of Fear* by Douglas J. Rumford

Doug Rumford's insightful book includes eight chapters specifically written to help you overcome eight common, everyday fears.

It explains how you can nurture your spiritual health by acknowledging your fears and strategically responding to them. You'll learn how to place your trust in God to break free from fear by awakening the courage of faith.

Plus, each chapter contains helpful follow-up questions as tools for personal reflection or group discussion.

**2** Enjoy listening to *For Those Who Need a Comforter* by Christine Wyrtzen

Another excellent resource is Christine Wyrtzen's inspirational music tape *For Those Who Need a Comforter.*

Christine's musical selections include eight songs specifically chosen to correspond to the eight weekly Adventure themes. Each song will comfort you as you face down your fears and anxieties with God's help.

Request your copy of *Scared to Life* or *For Those Who Need a Comforter* today! Use the order form on page 78 in this journal for convenient home delivery, or ask for these resources at your church or local Christian bookstore.

# *Friday, Date* ☐

*Read Philippians 4:4–9.*

1.   The subtitle of this Adventure is "Finding Courage When Anxiety Grips the Heart." What do verses 6–7 say we should do when we feel anxious?

_____

_____

2.   As you begin this 50-day series, what are some anxieties or fears you would like to face down?

_____

_____

3.   Verse 6 highlights two elements of prayer: petition (request) and thanksgiving. Why are both important when facing down our fears? Which of these would you like to see developed more in your prayer life?

_____

_____

4.   What promises does Paul give in these verses?

_____

_____

5.   One of the disciplines of this Adventure is to pray daily about areas of your life where you're not at peace. Read the prayer on page 8. How will using the prayer daily help you live out the principles of today's passage?

_____

_____

*God's Word is a practical manual for facing down our fears. We learn to understand the true nature of fear and the true source of power to overcome.* Douglas J. Rumford, *Scared to Life*, pp. 19–20

☐   I have read the introductory material on pages 3–13.

☐   I have looked over the eight Scripture memory passages on page 7.

☐   I have read the Facing Down Our Fears Prayer on page 8.

# *Saturday, Date* ☐

*Read Luke 4:1–13.*

1.  What are the three ways the devil tempted Jesus?
    1. _____
    2. _____
    3. _____

2.  Each time the devil tempted Jesus, he responded by quoting Scripture. What does this indicate about the importance of knowing God's Word?

    _____

    _____

3.  During this Adventure you will be encouraged to memorize a few short passages of Scripture, to be used when facing down your fears. What comfort do you find knowing that Jesus was tempted and found strength in God's Word?

    _____

    _____

4.  The Facing Down Our Fears Prayer of this Adventure acknowledges that the enemy, the devil, tempts us. Review the prayer on page 8. How does recognizing the enemy's "M.O." *(modus operandi)* help put fear in perspective?

    _____

    _____

5.  Notice that the Adventure prayer involves quoting Scripture. How will that give you power to face down your fears?

    _____

    _____

☐ I have read the introductory material on pages 3–13.

☐ I have started memorizing my first Scripture passage and recording my progress on page 7.

☐ I have begun praying the Facing Down Our Fears Prayer (see p. 8).

# *Sunday, Date* ☐

TOPIC INTRODUCTION: This Sunday through Friday, Days 1–6, your journal will encourage you to focus on the One in control, so that you can face down the fear of a society that's breaking down.

*John 16:33* ◀── **Memory Verse Option**

1. Read John 13:1–5. This is also the setting for John 16:33. Describe the scene.

_____

2. If you had only a short time with your closest family and friends before your death, what would you talk about?

_____

Now reread John 16:33, realizing these were some of the last words Jesus would share with his beloved disciples.

3. The context for "these things" in John 16:33 begins in chapter 13. Skim through chapters 13–16 and note some of the important concepts Jesus wants his disciples to remember.

_____

_____

4. Notice that Jesus says he is telling the disciples these things "so that in me you may have peace." What does it mean to have peace in Christ?

_____

5. What are three specific fears you have about our society? As believers, what basis do we have for taking courage in the midst of our fears?

    1. _____

    2. _____

    3. _____

_____

☐ I have read the introductory material on pages 3–13.

☐ I have begun praying the Facing Down Our Fears Prayer (p. 8).

☐ I am memorizing _____ and recording my progress on page 7.

☐ I have started to read chapters 1–2 of *How to Fear God Without Being Afraid of Him.*

# Monday, Date ☐

*Read Psalm 112.*

1. Verses 1 and 10 contrast two kinds of people. Who are they?

_____

_____

2. Verses 2–9 describe benefits of being one who fears the Lord. List some of those benefits.

_____

_____

3. Today's news reports are filled with events that could strike fear in our heart. How might verses 7–8 be reassuring?

_____

_____

4. The psalmist assumes the power of God to bless and protect those who fear him. Do you share that assumption at this point in your life? Why or why not?

_____

_____

5. On a scale of 1 to 10 (10 being complete calm), how would you rate your response to the direction of our society?

**1    2    3    4    5    6    7    8    9    10**

If you have a high rating, how would it change if you lived in a different area? Have a conversation with God and ask to experience his peace more fully.

_____

☐ I have read the introductory material on pages 3–13.

☐ I have begun praying the Facing Down Our Fears Prayer (p. 8).

☐ I am memorizing _____ and recording my progress on page 7.

☐ I have started to read chapters 1–2 of *How to Fear God Without Being Afraid of Him.*

# Tuesday, Date ☐

*Read Deuteronomy 34:5–Joshua 1:9.*

1.   Put yourself in the place of the Israelites at that time. You've just lost the only national leader you've ever known. List three fears that might characterize your response to the situation.

Afraid that _____

Afraid that _____

Afraid that _____

2.   What promises does God make to Joshua? What commands does God give Joshua? What do these commands and promises say about God's desires for Israel?

_____

_____

3.   In verses 7–8 Joshua is told to meditate on and obey the Book of the Law. Why do you think that was important? What motivation do you draw from verses 7–8 as you begin memorizing Scripture for this Adventure?

_____

_____

4.   Ultimately Joshua's success would not depend on his own efforts but on God. Do you believe that to be true for you when you feel fearful or insecure? What is one situation that you can trust the Lord with today?

_____

_____

5.   Who is a person you know who has faced down fear with God's courage? What is one lesson you can learn from him or her?

_____

_____

☐   I have read the introductory material on pages 3–13.

☐   I have prayed the Facing Down Our Fears Prayer (see p. 8).

☐   I am memorizing _____ and recording my progress on page 7.

☐   I have started to read chapters 1–2 of *How to Fear God Without Being Afraid of Him.*

# *Wednesday, Date* [ ]

*Read 2 Chronicles 20:1–17.*

1.  When Jehoshaphat faced the threat of physical invasion and subsequent foreign oppression, what was the progression of his response (see verse 3)?

    1. <u>Alarmed (afraid)</u>

    2. _____

    3. _____

2.  What would be your response if you learned that an army was coming to take over your country or community?

    _____

    _____

3.  What did God say through Jahaziel to calm the people (verse 17)?

    _____

    _____

4.  North American Christians are not challenged by the same kind of battle Jehoshaphat faced. What enemies do we face?

    _____

    _____

5.  How can you face down the fear of these enemies? How can your church do the same?

    _____

    _____

*We will come under attack from the world, the flesh, and the devil. When we fix our eyes on the Lord, resting them on the horizon point of faith, the soul sickness of fear subsides and our strength and courage rise.* Douglas J. Rumford, *Scared to Life,* p. 28

☐   I have read the introductory material on pages 3–13.

☐   I have prayed the Facing Down Our Fears Prayer (see p. 8).

☐   I am memorizing _____ and recording my progress on page 7.

☐   I am reading chapters 1–2 of *How to Fear God Without Being Afraid of Him.*

*Read Psalm 11.*

1.   When the psalmist David is in a fearful situation, what advice is he given by his peers (verses 1b– 3)?

_____

_____

2.   David chooses to face down his fears by taking refuge in the Lord. According to verses 4–7, what is his rationale for making that choice?

_____

_____

3.   Verse 2 talks about people who "shoot from the shadows at the upright in heart." Do you think that still happens today? In what ways have you experienced that kind of attack?

_____

_____

4.   Five days into this Adventure, you have started to memorize Scripture and make it part of your prayer life. How is doing that helping you take refuge in the Lord?

_____

_____

5.   The very last line of this psalm is a promise David relies on. How does it encourage you?

_____

_____

*Turnabout is God's play—even with the evil deeds of wicked men and women. God can and does take human evil and turn it inside out for His glory. What a dazzling God we serve!* Steve Halliday, *No Night Too Dark,* pp. 121–122

☐   I have read the introductory material on pages 3–13.

☐   I have prayed the Facing Down Our Fears Prayer (see p. 8).

☐   I am memorizing _____ and recording my progress on page 7.

☐   I am reading chapters 1–2 of *How to Fear God Without Being Afraid of Him.*

# *Friday, Date* ☐

*Read Philippians 2:12–16.*

1.  Paul writes that the Philippian Christians are living among a "crooked and depraved generation." Would you use similar words to describe our society? Why or why not?

_____

_____

2.  The Philippians are urged to "shine like stars in the universe as you hold out the word of life." How would you have interpreted those words?

_____

_____

3.  Which of these phrases comes closest to describing you? Your church?
    __ Fearful and withdrawn
    __ Courageous and influential
    __ Other _____
What is an example that explains your answer?

_____

_____

4.  One way Paul indicates we can influence our society is by being blameless and pure. Do you believe your behavior is evidence that you are a Christian? How can you consciously witness through your actions?

_____

_____

5.  How could you "hold out the word of life" to non-Christians? Add your own ideas to this list:
    __ Tell someone you're praying for him or her
    __ Look for opportunities to turn conversations toward God

__ _____

__ _____

__ _____

☐  I have prayed the Facing Down Our Fears Prayer (see p. 8).

☐  I am memorizing _____ and recording my progress on page 7.

☐  I have read chapters 1–2 of *How to Fear God Without Being Afraid of Him.*

On How to: **Focus on the One in Control to Overcome the Fear of a Society That's Breaking Down**

 **Read the following Scripture passages:**

Psalm 46
Romans 8:18–21
Philippians 1:27–30
Colossians 15:17

These Bible verses will give you additional helpful insights for learning how to turn to the Lord Almighty when you feel your world is spinning out of control.

**2** **Read this helpful book:**

*No Night Too Dark*
by Steve Halliday

We can all see, on television, in newspapers, and in our personal circumstances, how clearly our culture is spinning out of control—how sin in the world is contributing to the breakdown of society. But if you look closely and watch carefully you can also see God at work in our darkened world.

This inspiring book explains how God is capable of bringing light to your darkest nights by transforming apparent victories for Satan into glorious triumphs for his people. It will also teach you a divine principle: No matter how deep your pain, God can reach into your life and exchange suffering for glory.

Request your copy of *No Night Too Dark*. Use the order form on page 78 in this journal for convenient home delivery, or ask for the book at your church or local Christian bookstore.

TOPIC INTRODUCTION: This Saturday through Friday, Days 7–13, your journal will encourage you to live by God's standards of significance, so that you can face down the fear of living insignificant lives.

*Romans 8:15–16*    ◄── **Memory Verse Option**

1. In what different ways is the word *spirit* used in verses 15–16?

_____

_____

2. Are there any ways you may be a slave to fear? If so, what are they? Why, according to Paul, do we not need to be slaves to fear?

_____

_____

3. Paul writes that we've received the Spirit of sonship (or adoption). What emotions does that evoke in you?

_____

_____

4. When we fear insignificance, what proof could these verses give us that we are important to God?

_____

_____

5. The word *Abba* is Aramaic, the commonly spoken language in Israel in Jesus' time. The best English translation might be "Daddy." What does that indicate about the kind of relationship God has with his children, his chosen ones?

_____

_____

☐  I have prayed the Facing Down Our Fears Prayer today (p. 8).

☐  I am memorizing _____ and recording my progress on page 7.

☐  I have started to read chapters 3–4 of *How to Fear God Without Being Afraid of Him.*

*Read Esther 3:8–9; 4:1–17.*

1.    Esther didn't realize at first that God had given her a unique opportunity to do something significant. When have you been placed by God in a situation that allowed you to accomplish something you couldn't have done otherwise?

_____

_____

2.    In 4:16 Esther says, "If I perish, I perish." Do you see this as a statement of fear, of resignation, or of faith that God would intervene? Why?

_____

_____

3.    Has God placed you in a position to do something significant? What specifically do you think he might have in mind?

_____

_____

4.    Skim the rest of the Book of Esther to find out how the account ends. How does Esther's story challenge you to take advantage of opportunities God gives you?

_____

_____

5.    When reading this story, some would say it was lucky that Esther had come to her royal position. Do you think it was luck or something else? Explain your answer.

_____

_____

☐   I have prayed the Facing Down Our Fears Prayer today (see p. 8).

☐   I am memorizing _____ and recording my progress on page 7.

☐   I have started reading chapters 3–4 of *How to Fear God Without Being Afraid of Him.*

*Read Jeremiah 29:10–14.*

1.   These verses are part of a letter Jeremiah sent to the exiled Israelites in Babylon. If you had been captured, would you be skeptical about God's future plans for you? Why or why not?

_____

_____

2.   Even though the Israelites' circumstances were bad, God tells them they are still important to him. Has there been a time in your life when everything seemed to be going wrong and you questioned your significance to God? Explain.

_____

_____

3.   The Lord had marvelous future plans for Israel. Do you believe he has positive future plans for you? What might they be?

_____

_____

4.   When difficult situations arise, what is your usual response (i.e., worry, try to fix things, throw up your hands in frustration, etc.)? What specific response is suggested in verses 12–13?

_____

_____

5.   Sometimes we incorrectly think our significance can be measured by the degree to which God prospers us. What does it mean to find your significance in God? Explain your answer.

_____

_____

☐   I have prayed the Facing Down Our Fears Prayer today (see p. 8).

☐   I am memorizing _____ and recording my progress on page 7.

☐   I am reading chapters 3–4 of *How to Fear God Without Being Afraid of Him.*

*Read Galatians 2:17–21.*

1.   Reread verse 20 and put it in your own words.

_____

_____

2.   What is an aspect of your life that defines your significance? How does that compare with letting Christ live in and through you? Which is more important to you at this point?

_____

_____

3.   Would you characterize a life lived in total submission to Christ's desires as being significant or insignificant? Explain your answer.

_____

_____

4.   What struggles do you have in allowing Christ to live his life through you?

_____

_____

5.   In what circumstances do you sometimes fear you're living a life that has little significance? How does the truth of verse 20 address this fear?

_____

_____

*When we understand with our hearts, not just our minds, that we are handcrafted treasures, we begin to understand God's standards of significance. We were not created to earn value, but with value.* Douglas J. Rumford, *Scared to Life*, p. 44

☐   I have prayed the Facing Down Our Fears Prayer today (see p. 8).

☐   I am memorizing _____ and recording my progress on page 7.

☐   I am reading chapters 3–4 of *How to Fear God Without Being Afraid of Him.*

# *Thursday, Date* [        ]

*Read Micah 6:6–8.*

1.   Verses 6–7 indicate what the Israelites thought pleased God. Verse 8 reveals what God said would please him. Put verse 8 in your own words.

_____

_____

2.   Many times, people measure their significance by things they do. List three things you "do" for God.

1. _____

2. _____

3. _____

3.   How might the fear of living an insignificant life prompt you to try to prove your worth through actions?

_____

_____

4.   Walking humbly with our God means focusing on who we are in Christ, not exclusively on what we do. What is one way you can walk humbly with God today?

_____

5.   What are things our culture considers significant? In which direction do you find yourself being pulled most often: toward culture's view or toward God's view? Explain.

_____

_____

*Significance is not a search. It is a gift. When we receive full significance in Christ, we are liberated to live His significance through us and to enjoy His significant plans. This is our need. Only when we have been reunited with God through redemption will we discover the significance we were made to enjoy.* Joseph M. Stowell, *Perilous Pursuits,* p. 85

☐   I have prayed the Facing Down Our Fears Prayer today (p. 8).

☐   I am memorizing _____ and recording my progress on page 7.

☐   I am reading chapters 3–4 of *How to Fear God Without Being Afraid of Him.*

*Friday, Date* [          ]

*Read Matthew 10:29–31.*

1. In this passage, Jesus is sending out his disciples to minister. If you had been one of the disciples, what comfort would you have drawn from Jesus' words?

_____

_____

2. Many of the disciples had left all their worldly sources of significance (job, family, etc.) to follow Jesus. How do you think Jesus' words in these verses helped them redefine their significance?

_____

_____

3. What are areas in your life where you find significance?
   __ Position
   __ Family
   __ Relationships
   __ Skills
   __ Volunteer opportunities
   __ Other _____
   __ _____
   __ _____

4. If God called you to give up any of the above to follow him, what would that do to your sense of significance?

_____

_____

5. If Jesus were to speak verse 31 to you today, what words might he use?

_____

_____

☐ I have prayed the Facing Down Our Fears Prayer today (see p. 8).

☐ I am memorizing _____ and recording my progress on page 7.

☐ I have read chapters 3–4 of *How to Fear God Without Being Afraid of Him.*

On How to: **Live by God's Standards of Significance to Fight the Fear of Living Insignificant Lives**

 **Read the following Scripture passages:**

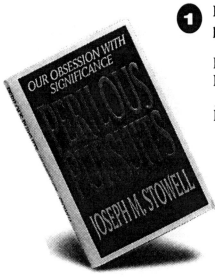

Ephesians 1:4–6
Ephesians 2:10
John 15:1–6
Isaiah 43:1–5

These Bible verses will give you additional helpful insights for focusing on Christ as your true source of meaning.

**Read this helpful book:**

*Perilous Pursuits*
by Joseph M. Stowell

While most committed Christians agree with the conclusion that "man's chief end is to glorify God and enjoy him forever," there are still many of us unconsciously consumed with glorifying ourselves or pursuing enjoyment apart from God.

This thought-provoking book explains why the pursuit of significance apart from God is "perilous" at best. Joseph Stowell will help you find personal fulfillment in surrendering to and serving Christ. Read this book and find the freedom that comes when you learn to live your life by God's standards of significance.

Request your copy of *Perilous Pursuits*. Use the order form on page 78 in this journal for convenient home delivery, or ask for the book at your church or local Christian bookstore.

TOPIC INTRODUCTION: This Saturday through Friday, Days 14–20, your journal will challenge you to draw courage from God's acceptance, so that you can face down the fear of rejection.

*Hebrews 13:6* ◄── **Memory Verse Option**

1.    Skim Hebrews 13. The author is giving a series of instructions. List a few from verses 1–5 and 7.

_____

_____

2.    Verses 5 and 6 cite two Old Testament passages, Deuteronomy 31:6 and Psalm 118:6–7. Read these passages and the surrounding verses. How do they shed light on today's verse?

_____

_____

3.    According to verse 6, the psalmist boasts that he is not afraid of what others might do to him because he knows who God is. How can reminding yourself of God's care be a help to you as you face down fears of rejection?

_____

_____

4.    Has there ever been a time when you were more scared about what people would think of you than about what God would think of you? Why was that? How did you handle it? How would you like to handle the fear of rejection if it arises again?

_____

_____

5.    Note that verse 5 urges Christians to be content with what they have. If we were truly content with what we have and with who we are, what would that do to our fear of rejection?

_____

☐    I have prayed the Facing Down Our Fears Prayer today (p. 8).

☐    I am memorizing _____ and recording my progress on page 7.

☐    I have started reading chapters 5–6 of *How to Fear God Without Being Afraid of Him*.

# *Monday, Date* ☐

*Read Acts 9:19b–28.*

1.  After nearly being killed for preaching Christ in Damascus (verses 23–25), what do you think Paul's response was when rejected by the disciples in Jerusalem?

_____

2.  Picture yourself in the disciples' situation today. A person responsible for the murder of some of your friends shows up at your church, claiming to have become a Christian. What are your thoughts about welcoming that person into your fellowship?

_____

3.  Paul's ministry would be tremendous. That may never have happened if Barnabas had not been courageous in befriending him. What does this say to you about the importance of encouraging someone this week?

_____

4.  Name a situation where you needed encouragement and someone risked rejection to reach out to you. What effect did this have on you?

_____

_____

5.  As you think about encouraging others for Discipline 4, do you have any fears? Ask God to give you Barnabas-like courage as you face down your fears and reach out to someone this week.

_____

☐ I have prayed the Facing Down Our Fears Prayer today (p. 8).

☐ I am thinking of people to be a Barnabas for (see p.10).

FRESHMAN ALVIN CLUNGLEY PROVES HE DOES HAVE THE GUTS TO ASK A GIRL FOR A DATE...

"Uh...when was the Declaration of Independence signed?"

# *Tuesday, Date* ⬜

*Read Proverbs 12:25.*

1.  Has there been a recent time when you had an anxious heart and someone cheered you up? What circumstances contributed to your anxiety? What did the person do to encourage you?

_____

_____

2.  Has anyone ever tried to encourage you with trite expressions? How did that make you feel? What do you think are essential elements of a truly "kind word"?

_____

_____

3.  Encouraging others can help us overcome the fear of being rejected. Look at Proverbs 12:18. What does this tell you about how not to encourage and how to encourage?

_____

_____

4.  Read Proverbs 16:24. A honeycomb was a precious commodity in ancient times. What does that suggest about the nature of pleasant words? Are they easy to obtain or give out?

_____

_____

5.  Having read about the power of an encouraging word, how does that challenge you to reach out to those who are weighed down?

_____

_____

☐ I have prayed the Facing Down Our Fears Prayer today (see p. 8).

☐ I am memorizing _____ and recording my progress on page 7.

☐ I am reading chapters 5–6 of *How to Fear God Without Being Afraid of Him.*

☐ I am thinking of people to be a Barnabas for (see p.10).

*Read Psalm 27.*

1.  David begins by asking two questions. Is he really seeking an answer, or does he already know the answer? How does this verse set the mood for the rest of the psalm?

_____

_____

2.  In verses 2–3 David lists personal attacks he has experienced. If you were writing this psalm today, what would you put in these verses?

_____

_____

3.  Compare verses 1–3 to verses 4–12. Is David more concerned with his relationship to others or his relationship to God? What about you?

_____

_____

4.  Judging by this psalm, did David think it was possible that God would reject him? That people would reject him? Do you fear rejection from God or people? Explain.

_____

_____

5.  In what specific area of your life do you fear rejection? How do David's words of confidence in God reassure you?

_____

_____

*God's acceptance enables us to keep human relationships, and especially the threat of rejection, in perspective. . . . In fact, our experience of God's approval enables us to cultivate a climate of acceptance and affirmation for others, who are often trapped in the fear of rejection.* Douglas J. Rumford, *Scared to Life*, pp. 55–56

☐    I have prayed the Facing Down Our Fears Prayer today (p. 8).

☐    I am memorizing _____ and recording my progress on page 7.

☐    I am reading chapters 5–6 of *How to Fear God Without Being Afraid of Him.*

☐    I have decided on someone to be a Barnabas for (p. 10).

*Read 2 Corinthians 1:3–4.*

1.   When is a time you have been comforted by God? According to these verses, how can God use that time in your life?

_____

2.   List three experiences you've had that may help you empathize with another's fear of rejection.
   1. _____
   2. _____
   3. _____

3.   Name a person who has comforted you in the past. What is one quality of that person's comfort that you would like to develop?

_____

4.   On a scale of 1 to 10 (10 being best), how good are you at comforting others?

**1     2     3     4     5     6     7     8     9     10**

Explain your rating. What can you do to improve?

_____

_____

5.   As you face down your fear of rejection and seek to encourage others, how do this week's verses challenge you?

_____

_____

*As we experience the deep sorrow of rejection and abandonment, our brokenness before God leads to a surrender of our stubborn, self-reliant will and paves the road for future faith-filled decisions that bring healing, acceptance, and nonpossessive love.* Carol Kent, *Tame Your Fears,* p. 131

☐   I have prayed the Facing Down Our Fears Prayer today (p. 8).

☐   I am memorizing _____ and recording my progress on page 7.

☐   I am reading chapters 5–6 of *How to Fear God Without Being Afraid of Him.*

☐   I have decided on someone to be a Barnabas for (p. 10).

*Friday, Date* ☐

*Read Psalm 56.*

1.   Turn to 1 Samuel 21:10–22:2 and read the context of what was happening to David when he wrote this psalm. What does this insight reveal about the intensity of verses 3–4?

_____

_____

2.   In verses 3–4, David seems to contrast the ideas of trusting in God and being afraid. Do you view them as opposing concepts? What does that say about your fears?

_____

_____

3.   David was facing considerable rejection at this point in his life. How can David's response to his situation encourage you when you feel rejected?

_____

_____

4.   Name someone you fear could reject you. Reread verse 4 (out loud), and insert the person's name in place of *man:*
     "What can _____ do to me?"
                        (name)

5.   In verse 8 David asks God not to overlook the anguish this situation is causing him. He seems to believe that God not only controls the physical situation, but that he cares also for the emotional stress it places David under. What does that say to you as you face down your fears of rejection?

_____

_____

☐   I have prayed the Facing Down Our Fears Prayer today
     (see p. 8).

☐   I am memorizing _____ and recording
     my progress on page 7.

☐   I have read chapters 5–6 of *How to Fear God Without Being
     Afraid of Him.*

☐   I have been a Barnabas for someone and recorded my progress
     on page 10.

On How to: **Draw Courage from God's Acceptance to Face Down the Fear of Rejection**

 **Read the following Scripture passages:**

Matthew 28:19–20
Acts 20:35
1 John 3:1
1 John 4:7–10

These Bible verses will help you to further focus on God's love and acceptance while you reach out to others in his name. When that occurs, you'll find the courage to make decisions that are faith-filled rather than fear-based.

**2** **Read this helpful book:**

*Tame Your Fears*
by Carol Kent

Written by an insightful Christian speaker and author, this practical book suggests ways you can tame 10 of the most common fears faced by Christian women today. You'll learn to move toward a more productive and satisfying future as you tame the fear of things that haven't yet happened, the fear of losing control, of being rejected, facing the past, and more.

Best of all, this book explains how you can use your fears as stepping-stones to a deeper faith, renewed confidence, and sincere reverence for our powerful but loving God. Women and men alike will appreciate Carol Kent's real-life illustrations and wise counsel.

Request your copy of *Tame Your Fears*. Use the order form on page 78 in this journal for convenient home delivery, or ask for the book at your church or local Christian bookstore.

TOPIC INTRODUCTION: This Saturday through Friday, Days 21–27, your journal will encourage you to discover true success by risking failure; so that you can face down the fear of the big "F" (failure).

*Psalm 37:23–24* ◄—— **Memory Verse Option**

1.  Skim Psalm 37. The author, David, is comparing two kinds of people. What are some characteristics of each?

_____

_____

2.  What would be a good subtitle for verses 23–26?

_____

3.  Skim 2 Samuel 11–12. How does knowing about David's weaknesses (stumblings) help you identify with these verses?

_____

4.  What are some things you're afraid of failing at? Have you ever really failed at them? Did it feel as though you stumbled, or did it feel as though you fell? What distinction is David making between stumbling and falling?

_____

_____

5.  Verse 24 in *The Living Bible* reads, "If they fall it isn't fatal, for the Lord holds them with his hand." How does knowing that the Lord holds you by the hand help you face down your fear of failure?

_____

_____

☐  I have prayed the Facing Down Our Fears Prayer today (p. 8).

☐  I am memorizing _____ and recording my progress on page 7.

☐  I have started reading chapters 7–8 of *How to Fear God Without Being Afraid of Him.*

☐  I have been a Barnabas for someone (see p. 10).

☐  I am deciding on an outrageously courageous act (see p. 41).

*Read Matthew 14:22–33.*

1.   At the beginning of this account, the disciples thought Jesus was a ghost, and they were afraid. What does verse 27 show about Jesus' compassion for his fearful disciples?

_____

2.   Looking carefully at verses 28–30, what caused Peter to sink? In verse 31, what does Jesus do, and what does he say to Peter?

_____

_____

3.   Notice in verse 32 that the wind, which caused Peter to fear, stopped when they got into the boat. Why do you think the wind didn't stop when Jesus first came on the scene? What did Peter learn about faith and failure?

_____

_____

4.   Do you think Peter intended to fail when he stepped out of the boat? Why was he distracted from Jesus? What does this story imply about the relationship between fear and failure?

_____

5.   When Peter said, "Lord, save me!" how did Jesus respond to his failure? This week you are to plan an "outrageously courageous act" for God (see p. 11). What comfort do you draw from Jesus' reaching out to Peter?

☐   I have prayed the Facing Down Our Fears Prayer today (p. 8).

☐   I am memorizing _____ and recording my progress on page 7.

☐   I have started reading chapters 7–8 of *How to Fear God Without Being Afraid of Him*.

☐   I have been a Barnabas for someone (see p. 10).

☐   I am deciding on an outrageously courageous act (see p. 41).

*Read 1 Samuel 17:1–50.*

1. The armies of Israel allowed Goliath to come out and taunt them day after day, perhaps because they were paralyzed by the fear of failure. In your life, when is a time you wanted to try something but were afraid? Looking back on that situation, what do you think about your fear?

_____

2. Based on verses 34–37, why was David not afraid of failing? List some events in your life that would be equivalent to the Lord's saving David from the lion and bear. How does looking at past victories help you face down fears of failing in the future?

_____

_____

3. It's important to note in verse 47 that David remembers who was responsible for his success. As you think about trying something new on God's behalf, how does it help you to know that success rests in his hands?

_____

4. David did not seem to focus on the possibility of failure, but on God's ability to give him victory. What tends to be your focus? Would you like to change that? If so, how?

_____

5. Most people would agree that fighting Goliath was an "outrageously courageous act." But not all such acts are done on that large a scale. Do you have a sense yet of what the Lord might be calling you to do as an outrageously courageous act? For help in preparation see page 41.

☐ I have prayed the Facing Down Our Fears Prayer today (p. 8).

☐ I am memorizing _____ and recording my progress on page 7.

☐ I am reading chapters 7–8 of *How to Fear God Without Being Afraid of Him.*

☐ I have been a Barnabas for someone and recorded my progress on page 10.

☐ I am deciding on an outrageously courageous act (see p. 41).

# DISCIPLINE 4

## Dare to Pull Off an Outrageously Courageous Act

### *Preparation*

Reread page 11. What are some things you normally wouldn't do, outrageously courageous acts, that you believe God is calling you to consider for this discipline? For example, think of areas in your life where you have felt prompted at times to do something, but were afraid.

__ Witnessing to a friend or family member
__ Getting to know people in your neighborhood or workplace
__ Volunteering with an organization
__ Teaching Sunday school
__ Singing or reading in your church service

__ _____
__ _____

What outrageously courageous act will you choose for this Adventure?

_____

What about your outrageously courageous act scares you?

_____

What preparations can you make that will help you be less afraid?

_____

Now that you have decided on what to do, begin planning. The first step is to go to God with your fear and ask him for courage. Then decide when you are going to do this act, and do it!

### *Evaluation*

Now that you have completed your outrageously courageous act, how did you do? Are you pleased with the results? Why or why not?

_____

Were you afraid of failing? If so, what do you think of that fear now?

_____

What have you learned from this discipline? How has it helped you to face down your fears and rely on God for courage? What might you do differently if you had it to do over again?

_____

You may want to continue with your outrageously courageous act. Also, you may want to review your list of ideas and try some more of them.

*Wednesday, Date* [＿＿＿＿]

*Read 2 Timothy 1:3–7.*

1.   What were some of the difficulties Timothy was facing? (Hint: Look at 1 Timothy 4:11–15 and 5:21–23.) Do you think Timothy felt he was failing or feared that he could fail? Why or why not?

_____

_____

2.   In 2 Timothy 1:6 Paul reminds Timothy to rekindle God's gift. The image is one of turning smoldering coals into a flaming blaze. Is there a spiritual gift of yours that needs rekindling? Has the fear of failure kept you from using this gift fully? If so, what can you do to change this situation?

_____

3.   Notice the contrast in verse 7 of qualities of spirit. Do you think of your spirit as being powerful, loving, and self-disciplined? Why or why not? If you truly believed these traits were part of your life, how would that affect your fear of failure?

_____

4.   List three areas of your life where you feel timid or cowardly at times. How does this passage speak to those fears?

   1._____

   2._____

   3._____

5.   Paul wrote this letter to Timothy while he was in prison awaiting execution. He didn't seem to be worried that Timothy would see him as a failure. Do you think Paul was a failure in the world's eyes? How about in God's eyes? What does that say to us about our fears of failure?

_____

☐   I have prayed the Facing Down Our Fears Prayer today (p. 8).

☐   I am memorizing _____ and recording my progress on page 7.

☐   I have started reading chapters 7–8 of *How to Fear God Without Being Afraid of Him.*

☐   I have decided on a second person to encourage (p. 10).

☐   I am planning my outrageously courageous act (see p. 41).

# *Thursday, Date* ☐

*Read Hebrews 4:14–16.*

1.  How do these verses indicate Christ views our weaknesses?

_____

2.  Has there been a time when you have found comfort in a trying time by knowing that Christ has gone through similar trials? Explain.

_____

_____

3.  When is a time you were especially aware of a personal weakness or failure? Were you able to approach God with confidence, as these verses suggest? Why or why not?

_____

_____

4.  According to verse 16, what does God offer us? How is it comforting to know ahead of time that God will be merciful when you approach him?

_____

_____

5.  How does this passage help put the fear of failure in perspective?

_____

_____

*The fear of failure robs us of tapping the deepest riches of life. Riches aren't mined on the surface. They require the risk of going deeper, of exploring uncharted territory, of "wasting time and resources" learning what doesn't work. The creative process of exploration can appear to be an extravagant waste—until we strike gold.* Douglas J. Rumford, *Scared to Life*, p. 73

☐   I have prayed the Facing Down Our Fears Prayer today (p. 8).

☐   I am memorizing _____ and recording my progress on page 7.

☐   I am reading chapters 7–8 of *How to Fear God Without Being Afraid of Him.*

☐   I have decided on a second person to encourage (see p. 10).

☐   I am planning my outrageously courageous act (see p. 41).

# *Friday, Date* ☐

*Read 1 Chronicles 28:20.*

1.   Skim chapter 28. What specifically is David encouraging Solomon about? How would you feel if you were in charge of building the structure that the very God of heaven was going to inhabit?

_____

2.   What is the reason Solomon is not to be discouraged? What is a task or responsibility in your life that you find overwhelming? How do David's words to Solomon encourage you?

_____

3.   Notice that David is instructing Solomon to couple the correct attitude (being courageous) with the correct action (building the temple). Do you tend to focus more on attitude or on action? Is there an area of your life where you need to balance the focus? Explain.

_____

_____

4.   Is there an area of service God might be calling you to perform on his behalf for which you need courage? What is it? With that in mind, reread this verse as if David were saying these words to you.

_____

5.   Perhaps the area of service you listed above will be your outrageously courageous act. What progress are you making? To read more about this Adventure discipline, see pages 11 and 41.

_____

*When we allow the fear of failure to dominate us, we are demanding a guaranteed outcome in the situation. But a guaranteed outcome takes away the opportunity to live by faith.* H. Norman Wright, *Afraid No More!*, p. 110

☐   I have prayed the Facing Down Our Fears Prayer today (p. 8).

☐   I am memorizing _____ and recording my progress on page 7.

☐   I have finished the book *How to Fear God Without Being Afraid of Him.*

☐   I have been a Barnabas for two people (see p. 10).

☐   I am planning my outrageously courageous act (see p. 41).

On How to: **Discover True Success by Risking Failure, to Face Down the Fear of the Big "F"**

 Read the following Scripture passages:

1 John 2:1–12
Matthew 11:28–30
John 15:5–6
Colossians 3:23–24

These Bible verses will give you further ideas on how to overcome crippling fears of failure by learning to step out in faith on God's behalf and become a true winner for Christ.

**2** Read this helpful book:

*Afraid No More!*
by H. Norman Wright

Have you ever put off doing something you really wanted to do because, deep down, you were afraid? If you have, Norman Wright can help. In this thoughtful and intelligent book, you'll discover how to overcome the unhealthy fears that keep you from living a full and confident life for Christ.

You'll learn to replace your fears with faith, gain confidence from God, live victoriously, and do the things God really wants you to do.

Request your copy of *Afraid No More!* Use the order form on page 78 in this journal for convenient home delivery, or ask for the book at your church or local Christian bookstore.

TOPIC INTRODUCTION: This Saturday through Friday, Days 28–34, your journal will encourage you to set aside distorted views of God, so that you can face down the unhealthy fear of God.

*Psalm 103:13*  ◄— **Memory Verse Option**

1. Read all of Psalm 103. What is the general tone? (Start by looking at words that tell what God does and what he's like.)

_____

2. How does the picture of God that David paints in verse 13 compare to the model of your earthly father?

_____

3. Some people fear that God is an overcritical Father and are afraid of his disapproval. How does this psalm address that fear?

_____

4. In verse 14 we see that God understands our humanity. What does that indicate about his compassion?

_____

5. What are possible unhealthy fears of God that you may have? Do you relate to any of these distorted views?
    __ God as an overcritical teacher expecting perfection
    __ God as an absentee father too busy for me
    __ God as a no-nonsense boss—always serious and never fun
    __ God as an abusive parent not concerned with my well-being
    __ a God who wants to take advantage of his power over me
    __ a God who is angry and resentful, wanting to get even with me
    __ Other _____

Pray that God will help you face down any unhealthy fears of him.

☐ I have prayed the Facing Down Our Fears Prayer today (p. 8).

☐ I am memorizing _____ and recording my progress on page 7.

☐ I have done the outrageously courageous act preparation exercises on page 41.

# *Monday, Date* [            ]

*Read Luke 15:11–32.*

1.   The younger son made some very unwise decisions regarding his resources and relationships, which hurt others and himself. Which character in this parable do you most identify with? Why?

_____

2.   How do you suppose the younger son expected to be treated by his family when he returned? Do you think he was afraid when he first decided to return to his father?

_____

3.   In light of the son's wanderings, what makes the father's welcome so special?

_____

4.   How does your view of God compare with the picture of the father painted by Christ in this parable?

_____

5.   How could thinking of God as a Father who welcomes home his wayward children help you overcome an unhealthy fear of him?

_____

_____

*The fear of the Lord is that deep and abiding sense of appreciation and love for God which inspires me to live in a manner that reflects my devotion and respect for God and God's will. Because of the depth of his love and sacrifice for me, I do not want to offend God or cause any reason for others to condemn His name. The fear of the Lord is the beginning of wisdom because it is the smartest way to live!* Douglas J. Rumford, *Scared to Life,* p. 98

☐   I have prayed the Facing Down Our Fears Prayer today (p. 8).

☐   I am memorizing _____ and recording my progress on page 7.

☐   I have been a Barnabas for two people and recorded my progress on page 10.

☐   I am planning a special meal to discuss the unhealthy fear of God (see p. 12).

*Read Micah 7:18–20.*

1.  List the characteristics of God revealed in this passage (hint: look at the verbs). How do these characteristics compare to how you view God?

_____

_____

2.  Has there been a time when you've feared that God's mercy and love for you were nonexistent, as if God were waiting to "really get you good"? Is that consistent with God's qualities described in this passage? Give one phrase from the passage to support your answer.

_____

3.  Is there a sin in your life for which you've had trouble believing God could forgive you? Reread verses 18–19 with that sin in mind. How does that make you feel?

_____

4.  What would you tell someone who you thought had an unhealthy fear of God? How could you use this passage to help calm the person's fear?

_____

_____

5.  As children, we learn about our heavenly Father through the example of our earthly parents. How does your parents' model affect your view of God? Are there any adjustments that need to be made in the way you relate to the Lord?

_____

_____

☐ I have prayed the Facing Down Our Fears Prayer today (p. 8).

☐ I am memorizing _____ and recording my progress on page 7.

☐ I have decided on a third person to encourage (see p. 10).

☐ I have done the outrageously courageous act exercises (p. 41).

# *Wednesday, Date* ☐

*Read Isaiah 49:13–16a.*

1.   What in these verses would be comforting to an Israelite nation taken captive by their enemies and fearing they had been rejected by God?

_____

_____

2.   Have you ever felt as if God had completely forsaken you? According to this passage, did God really forsake you? How could this help the next time you fear God has forgotten you?

_____

_____

3.   God compares his love for his people with the love of a mother for her young child. What does it mean to you to know that God's love is even stronger?

_____

_____

4.   What does Isaiah mean when he says God has engraved us on his palms? If you were writing this passage today, how would you express the same idea?

_____

_____

5.   How does knowing that God is ever-present help you face down your unhealthy fears of God?

_____

_____

☐   I have prayed the Facing Down Our Fears Prayer today (p. 8).

☐   I am memorizing _____ and recording my progress on page 7.

☐   I have decided on a third person to encourage and recorded my progress on page 10.

☐   I have completed my outrageously courageous act and evaluated my effort on page 41.

☐   I am planning a special meal to discuss the unhealthy fear of God (see p. 12).

# *Thursday, Date* ☐

*Read Zephaniah 3:14–17.*

1. Why, according to Zephaniah, is there cause for great rejoicing?

_____

2. What picture is painted of God in verse 17? Is this a conception of God that you either overlook or overemphasize? Why might that be?

_____

_____

3. Notice the protective nature of God revealed in verse 15. How would you rate your own sense of confidence in God's protection? How could you improve that?

_____

_____

4. In what ways have you seen God's protection in your life? Does remembering his protection help you to face down unhealthy fears?

_____

_____

5. Picture God rejoicing over you with singing (verse 17). What song might he sing?

_____

*There are two parts of fear—the regard and the distance. . . . It is the distance that is abolished by God's love. He reaches out to us and pulls us close. We retain a healthy regard—a "fear," if you want to call it that—of his power and righteousness. But we can relax a bit in the acceptance we find in Christ.* David New and Randy Petersen, *How to Fear God Without Being Afraid of Him*, pp. 17–18

☐ I have prayed the Facing Down Our Fears Prayer today (p. 8).

☐ I am memorizing _____ and recording my progress on page 7.

☐ I have completed my outrageously courageous act and evaluated my effort on page 41.

☐ I have scheduled a special meal to discuss the unhealthy fear of God (see p. 12).

*Read Proverbs 9:10.*

1. Review the checklist for question 5 on page 46. How do the verses from the past week and Proverbs 9:10 shed light on the unhealthy fear of God? What is a correct view?

_____

_____

2. To fear God appropriately, why is it essential to have a correct understanding of him?

_____

3. Look at Proverbs 16:6. According to this verse, what is the relationship between avoiding evil and the fear of the Lord? Does *fear* mean "to be scared" in this verse? If not, what words could you use to help you understand what is meant by *fear* in this verse?

_____

_____

4. Read Proverbs 19:23 and compare it to Zephaniah 3:15. Both passages show God's protection over his people. How can concentrating on God's protection help counteract the unhealthy fear of him?

_____

_____

5. Has your understanding of the fear of the Lord changed during this Adventure? How have you grown in wisdom or peace?

_____

_____

☐   I have prayed the Facing Down Our Fears Prayer today (p. 8).

☐   I am memorizing _____ and recording my progress on page 7.

☐   I have read *How to Fear God Without Being Afraid of Him.*

☐   I have been a Barnabas for three people and recorded my progress on page 10.

☐   I have completed my outrageously courageous act and evaluated my effort on page 41.

On How to: **Set Aside Distorted Views of God to Clear Up the Unhealthy Fear of God**

**1** **Read the following Scripture passages:**

James 4:7–8; John 1:18; John 14:9–10;1 Peter 5:6–7

These Bible verses will give you additional helpful insights on developing a balanced perspective of the true nature of God. You'll discover that while God is powerful and holy, he is also loving and desires to have a close personal relationship with you.

**2** **Read this helpful book:**

*How to Fear God Without Being Afraid of Him* by David New and Randy Petersen

Why do so many Christians enter God's kingdom but remain in the doorway? Maybe we fear God's judgment when we should be enjoying his love. Maybe we remain chained to the ground when we should be soaring on eagle's wings.

But whether our fear of God was once healthy and has now turned oppressive, or whether our fear has grown out of ignorance or wrong teachings, it is time to grow up into love.

This book will teach you to enjoy God's love by balancing your understanding of his power and holiness with his desire for an intimate relationship with you.

**Request your copy of *How to Fear God Without Being Afraid of Him*. Use the order form on page 78 in this journal for convenient home delivery, or ask for the book at your church or local Christian bookstore. Also available on audiocassette.**

**3** **Read this added devotional material:**

On the next page you'll find a follow-up page from the Scripture Union devotional series *Discovery*. This particular page of devotional thoughts relates to the subject of facing down the unhealthy fear of God. It will help you realize that the God who controls nature shows deep care for you.

# Faith That Keeps Us Safe

*FACING DOWN THE UNHEALTHY FEAR OF GOD*

 **Pray** Increase my faith, Lord, as I study today, knowing that you and your promises never change.

 **Read** The story of Joshua and his people crossing the Jordan reminds us of Moses leading them across the Red Sea (Exodus 14:21-29). These events weren't just spectacular miracles: they were a test of obedience. God's presence kept them safe.

**NOW READ: JOSHUA 3:1–17.**

 **Reflect** How was it possible for the Israelites to cross the river Jordan?

God's power over nature was a great source of encouragement for Old Testament writers. The psalmist recalls the events of Joshua 3 with thanksgiving (Psalm 66:6); there's God's promise in Isaiah: "When you pass through the waters, I will be with you" (Isaiah 43:2); and later, Jesus rebukes his disciples for not trusting him to protect them on a stormy lake (Luke 8:24–25).

What is your response to the might of God? Is it a feeling of awe, of anxiety, of perhaps even fear? Whatever we're doing today we needn't be afraid that God will harm or abandon us or allow us to be overwhelmed by our troubles. The God who held back the Jordan waters will keep us safe from whatever we're afraid of. If it is God himself we fear, we need only to understand his major concern: that we honor and glorify him with our lives. He longs for a close relationship with us and promises he will be there to comfort and encourage us in difficult circumstances. All he asks is that, like the Israelites, we're prepared for him to act (5) and are ready to do what he wants.

 **Apply** "The Lord will keep you from all harm—he will watch over your life; the Lord will watch over your coming and going...forevermore" (Psalm 121:7–8). How can this help you today—at work, at school, or wherever you may be?

 **Pray** Thank you, Lord, that "even though I walk through the valley of the shadow of death, I will fear no evil, for you are with me" (Psalm 23:4).

To order *Discovery* or other age-graded Scripture Union devotional resources see the order form on page 76.

TOPIC INTRODUCTION: This Saturday through Friday, Days 35–41, your journal will encourage you to learn to trust in God's sufficiency, so that you can face down the fear of sickness, aging, and death.

*Psalm 23:4*   ◄— **Memory Verse Option**

1.   Read through all of Psalm 23. What characteristics of a good shepherd are highlighted here?

_____

_____

2.   A shepherd had the responsibility of protecting, providing for, guiding, and nurturing the flock. How have you seen God exercising these responsibilities in your life recently?

_____

_____

3.   If someone wrote a psalm like this today, what might be a modern-day equivalent of the shepherd?

_____

4.   In verse 4 the psalmist David says, "I walk . . ." but there is also someone else in the valley of the shadow of death. Who is it? In what ways can the promise of God's presence give you courage as you face down fears of sickness, aging, and death?

_____

_____

5.   For the shepherd, the rod was used to defend the sheep from wild animals, and the staff was used to keep the sheep in line and guide them. Why do you think these "tools" gave David comfort? How might they comfort you?

_____

_____

☐  I have prayed the Facing Down Our Fears Prayer today (p. 8).

☐  I am memorizing _____ and recording my progress on page 7.

☐  I have scheduled a special meal to discuss the unhealthy fear of God (see p. 12).

# *Monday, Date* [　　　]

*Read Lamentations 3:19–26.*

1.  In the midst of affliction, what reason does the author, Jeremiah, have to be hopeful?

_____

_____

2.  When is a time your soul was downcast? Were you able to focus on God's love and compassion? In situations like these, how does it help to remember that God's mercies are fresh every day?

_____

_____

3.  What are some specific ways you could call to mind God's mercies in difficult times?
    _ Read Scripture
    _ Meditate on a memory verse
    _ Write down three things you're thankful for
    _ Sing a hymn or chorus of praise
    _ Recall times God has provided for you in the past
    _ Other _____

4.  This week we're considering the fear of sickness, aging, and death. Do these verses help you entrust your fears to God? Why or why not?

_____

_____

5.  Do you know someone sick or infirm who might need encouragement? How could you be an instrument of God's mercy for that person this week?

_____

_____

☐ I have prayed the Facing Down Our Fears Prayer today (see p. 8).

☐ I am memorizing _____ and recording my progress on page 7.

☐ I have scheduled a special meal to discuss the unhealthy fear of God (see p. 12).

*Tuesday, Date* ☐

*Read 2 Corinthians 12:7–10.*

1.    What was God's response to Paul's request for relief from his thorn i
the flesh? Do you find this surprising? Why or why not?

_____

_____

2.    One of the fears of becoming physically weak is the possibility that
we'll lose our ability to work, care for our loved ones, and so on. In what
ways does this passage speak to that fear?

_____

_____

3.    When faced with limitations, we're often forced to rely more heavily
on God. When has that been true in your experience?

_____

_____

4.    Do you have fears related to sickness, aging, and death—for yourself
and your loved ones? Do God's words to Paul in this passage comfort you
Why or why not?

_____

_____

5.    Think of a person you know who has a physical weakness. Based on
this passage, how does God see him or her? Does that change the way you
view this person? If so, how?

_____

_____

☐    I have prayed the Facing Down Our Fears Prayer today
     (see p. 8).

☐    I am memorizing _____ and recording
     my progress on page 7.

☐    I completed my outrageously courageous act and evaluated my
     effort on page 41.

☐    I have scheduled a special meal to discuss the unhealthy fear c
     God (see p. 12).

# *Wednesday, Date* ☐

*Read Psalm 92:12–15.*

1.   According to the psalmist, righteousness is the necessary ingredient for a productive life. How does that compare to the way our culture views productivity?

_____

2.   Does our society honor senior citizens or denigrate them? How does that compare with the message of this psalm?

_____

3.   As you grow older, what are some of the lifestyle changes you fear?

_____

_____

4.   Based on this psalm, what are some preparations you could make to ensure you're still productive in old age?

_____

_____

5.   How does this passage help you face down fears related to aging?

_____

*Where fear makes human suffering a barrier to the fullness of life, faith can make it a bridge to the presence, peace, and power of God.* Douglas J. Rumford, *Scared to Life,* p. 106

☐   I have prayed the Facing Down Our Fears Prayer today (p. 8).

☐   I am memorizing _____ and recording my progress on page 7.

**"Dee Dee Vershay's dog is having a hernia operation.
Everybody's signing this get-well card and kicking in $10."**

*Read John 11:17–27.*

1.   What do these verses communicate about Jesus' power when it comes to life and death?

_____

_____

2.   Why do we fear death? Does knowing that God is in control over life and death comfort you? Why or why not?

_____

_____

3.   Read verses 28–36. Why do you think Jesus wept? What does that show about his compassion for his people?

_____

_____

4.   In verses 25–26, what kind of life is Jesus talking about: mortal or immortal? At the end of verse 26, Jesus asks Martha, "Do you believe this?" What would you say if Jesus asked that of you? Why?

_____

_____

5.   How does Jesus' promise in these verses help calm your fears related to death?

_____

_____

*Sometimes God seemed silent, and I slipped easily into despair. Occasionally, though, when I needed it most, someone would reach out to me—someone like the friend who wept with me that first day. During those times I was consoled to my depths and reassured that God was alive and taking care of me.* Christine Wyrtzen, *Carry Me*

☐   I have prayed the Facing Down Our Fears Prayer today (see p. 8).

☐   I am memorizing _____ and recording my progress on page 7.

☐   I have had a special meal and discussed the unhealthy fear of God with family and friends.

# *Friday, Date* ☐

*Read Luke 2:21–38.*

1. This passage reveals a high regard for senior citizens. List some of the characteristics of Anna and Simeon highlighted in these verses.

_____

_____

2. Do you think Simeon and Anna were in a better or worse position than some of the younger people to recognize Jesus as the Messiah? Why? What does that say about age and senior citizens today?

_____

_____

3. Do you know an older person with spiritual maturity like Simeon or Anna? What could you learn from that person's example? (You may even ask the person to tell you about his or her spiritual journey.)

_____

4. Some people fear the loss of people to love or significant tasks to perform. God still works through people in their old age. How do the examples of Anna and Simeon help dispel your fears of becoming insignificant when you grow older?

_____

5. Simeon was not afraid to die, because he had seen the Messiah. Verses 29–32 are sometimes called the Song of Simeon. Write a few words that express your own feelings about one day seeing the Lord.

_____

_____

☐ I have prayed the Facing Down Our Fears Prayer today (p. 8).

☐ I am memorizing _____ and recording my progress on page 7.

☐ I have had a special meal and discussed the unhealthy fear of God with family or friends.

On How to: **Trust in God's Sufficiency for Dealing with the Fear of Sickness, Aging, and Death**

 **Read the following Scripture passages:**

1 Corinthians 15:54–57; Hebrews 2:14–15; Revelation 21:4; John 14:1–4, 27

These Bible verses will help remind you that no matter what your age or physical condition you remain significant before God. When you trust in the Father of all comfort, you'll find courage to move through life, traversing hills and valleys with confidence.

 **Read this helpful book:**

*Carry Me* by Christine Wyrtzen

You'll deeply appreciate this touching personal story by Christian recording artist Christine Wyrtzen.

In this book Christine shares a sensitive firsthand account of her mother's illness and subsequent death to cancer. If you have ever struggled with fears about sickness, aging, or death you will find comfort in her story. Christine also offers tangible hope for those in the shadows of a personal life crisis. This book will strike a responsive chord with anyone facing a dark road ahead.

Request your copy of *Carry Me*. Use the order form on page 78 in this journal for convenient home delivery, or ask for the book at your church or local Christian bookstore.

 **Read this added devotional material:**

On the next page you'll find a follow-up page from the Scripture Union devotional series *Discovery*. This particular page of devotional thoughts relates to the subject of facing down the fear of sickness, aging, and death. It will help you see that God is always in control, even over life and death situations.

# Confidence During Crisis

*FACING DOWN THE FEAR OF SICKNESS, AGING, AND DEATH*

 **Pray**   Father, as I study your Word today, may I be thrilled anew with your power over death.

 **Read**   Jesus is going to die on the cross—the ultimate test of his Father's power to bring him through agony to the promised glory. We tend to forget that Jesus was fully human as well as fully God. He needed friends like this family at Bethany.

**NOW READ: JOHN 11:1–16.**

 **Reflect**   Why did Jesus delay going to the home of his sick friend, Lazarus (14)?

The word comes. "Your friend is ill." Jesus immediately talks about death. But God was going to work a miracle.
- What seems like total disaster in life can be used by God for his purposes and for our eventual gain (4). It seemed like a tragedy for Martha and Mary *at the time*. Later they would recall it with wonder and joy. Don't be in a hurry to assess the meaning of the events in your life: God is in them.
- When we submit our lives to God, we become part of his timetable for the world and can be absolutely sure that his timing is right (9–10). Jesus was coming near to the end of his "day," but he had nothing to fear.
- Death becomes "sleep" when Jesus is in charge (12–13). And there is all the difference between the two.
- Thomas's faith may have been less than perfect (16); but there was no doubt about his courage and his devotion to Jesus. Without that hard core of courage and commitment, faith can easily degenerate into a kind of religious cotton candy.

 **Apply**   When we confront sickness, aging, and death, we need to base our resolve on the solid foundation of God's Word and a strong faith in his Son. How can you draw strength from Scripture to help you or a loved one face down these fears?

 **Pray**   May the words of faith that I sing and speak always be backed up by readiness to act, and, if need be, to suffer for your sake, Lord.

To order *Discovery* or other age-graded Scripture Union devotional resources see the order form on page 76.

TOPIC INTRODUCTION: This Saturday through Wednesday, Days 42–46, your journal will encourage you to help equip children with God's resources, so that you can face down the fear of threats to our children.

*Psalm 103:17* ◄— **Memory Verse Option**

1. According to Psalm 103:17, who receives the benefit when believers fear God?

_____

_____

2. Read verses 15–16. In that context, why do you think David starts verse 17 with "from everlasting to everlasting"?

_____

_____

3. The word for love used in verse 17 also appears in the refrains of Psalm 136. Read through that psalm. What do you learn about God's love that sheds light on this memory verse? Write down a few of your ideas.

_____

_____

4. This week we are facing down the fear of threats to our children. According to Psalm 103, our earthly lives are fleeting. How does it encourage you to know that God's love for children's children is eternal?

_____

_____

5. Based on verses 17–18, how should we go about ensuring our children's future? What is a specific way you can do that for children in your life?

_____

_____

☐ I have prayed the Facing Down Our Fears Prayer today (see p. 8).

☐ I am memorizing _____ and recording my progress on page 7.

# Monday, Date ☐

*Read Matthew 21:14–16.*

1.   Turn to Psalm 8:1–2. In this psalm, which talks about the grandeur of God, notice the role children play. Have you generally thought of children as playing an extremely important role in the worship of God? What do these verses say?

_____

_____

2.   If children are "ordained" into God's plan, what does this indicate about their future (i.e., how important their future is to God)?

_____

_____

3.   Note the two groups of people in the Matthew passage. One is a group of teachers and the other a group of children. How do their responses to Jesus differ? Why is that a surprise, given the training and background of the two groups?

_____

_____

4.   Children usually have little say over what happens to them, yet in these verses they make a stirring pronouncement. How could children be more involved in the life of your community of faith?

_____

_____

5.   When you think about threats to our children's future, what are you most afraid of? Why? How do today's passages speak to your fears?

_____

_____

☐   I have prayed the Facing Down Our Fears Prayer today (see p. 8).

☐   I am memorizing _____ and recording my progress on page 7.

☐   I have been a Barnabas for three people and recorded my progress on page 10.

*Read Mark 10:13–16.*

1.    Why do you think the disciples rebuked the people for bringing their children to Jesus? What does this behavior reveal about the disciples' view of children?

_____

_____

2.    Jesus got angry with his disciples. What does this reveal about his concern for the children? How does that make you feel?

3.    When we are told to receive the kingdom of God like a little child, what does that mean? Are there areas in your life where you need a more childlike faith? If so, what are they?

_____

_____

4.    How does Jesus' love and compassion for children in this passage help you face down fears of threats to our children today?

_____

5.    What are some ways you could impact children for Christ?

_____

_____

*We will overcome our fear for the next generation as we better understand their perspective on life, encourage them with God's vision of hope, and empower them with the resources of God's Good News.* Douglas J. Rumford, *Scared to Life,* p. 124

☐    I have prayed the Facing Down Our Fears Prayer today (p. 8).

*"FOR CRYIN' OUT LOUD MOM! IT'S ONLY A SLIDE!"*

*Read Proverbs 22:6.*

1.   In *The Living Bible*, this proverb reads, "Teach a child to choose the right path." What are some key elements of that kind of training?

_____

_____

2.   According to this verse, what is the result of training a child in the right way? Does this proverb reassure you or scare you? Why?

_____

_____

3.   Do you ever fear that you don't have the ability to do what this verse says? What is one step you could take to begin to face down this fear?
   __ Go to someone for advice
   __ Read about working with children
   __ Ask God for wisdom
   __ Other _____

4.   Who in your life was most influential in training you in the right way? What is one quality of that person you'd like to emulate?

_____

5.   Usually when a baby is dedicated or baptized, the church is asked to take some responsibility for the child's welfare. How well do you think your church is fulfilling that charge? How seriously do you as a church member take this responsibility?

_____

*It was God's power that enabled my family to make it when my brother came home with the shocking news that his girlfriend was pregnant. It is God's power that has enabled parents to keep going after the death of a child. . . . God's providence, promises, presence, and power make a compelling case for us to learn to rely on Him.*
Jack and Jerry Schreur, *Family Fears*, pp. 179–180

☐   I have prayed the Facing Down Our Fears Prayer today (p. 8).
☐   I have memorized five Scripture passages and recorded my progress on page 7.

On How to: **Equip Our Children with God's Resources, to Overcome the Fear of Threats to Our Children**

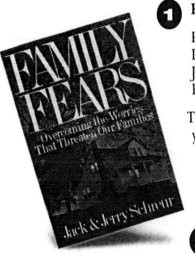

**1** **Read the following Scripture passages:**

Psalm 139:13–16
Deuteronomy 6:4–7
James 1:5
Psalm 4

These Bible verses will further encourage you to commit your loved ones to God and entrust them to his care. When you do, you'll find that your concerns for their welfare will not develop into paralyzing fears and anxieties.

**2** **Read this helpful book:**

*Family Fears* by Jack and Jerry Schreur

This book offers you solid Scripture-based strategies for breaking the cycle of fear that can paralyze a Christian home. Included are discussions on dealing with the five most common family fears.

Fear does not have to dominate your life. This book will show you how to cultivate an environment of confident love and acceptance by entrusting your family to God's care.

**3** **Pick up this special video:**

*Veggie Tales: Where's God When I'm Scared?* by Big Idea Productions

This wonderful family video features animated vegetables that teach your youngsters how they are always safe and secure in the hands of God. It's great video entertainment with a solid Christian message on how children can overcome their fears.

Request your copy of *Family Fears* or the *Where's God When I'm Scared?* Video. Use the order form on page 78 in this journal for convenient home delivery, or ask for these resources at your church or local Christian bookstore.

# *Thursday, Date* ☐

**TOPIC INTRODUCTION:** This Thursday through Sunday, Days 47–50, your journal will encourage you to find confidence in the risen Lord, so that you can face down the fear of the rise of evil.

*Read John 17:13–19.*

1.   This is the last prayer the disciples would hear from Jesus, so his words took on special importance. Look carefully at this passage and list Jesus' specific requests.

_____

_____

2.   Notice that Jesus asks God to protect his disciples from the evil one. What does that indicate about the evil one's power and influence?

_____

3.   Jesus expects that his disciples will continue to be greeted by opposition. Are you surprised when Christians are met with opposition today? Why or why not?

_____

_____

4.   As Jesus anticipated his crucifixion, he knew his disciples would face evil as well. During this fearful time, do you think they felt protected, as Jesus had asked? (Skim John 18–20 for help.) Were they truly protected?

_____

_____

5.   What fears of evil might plague Christians today?

_____

_____

6.   Read verse 20. How is it comforting to know that even while he was on earth Jesus prayed for future believers like us?

_____

_____

☐   I have prayed the Facing Down Our Fears Prayer today (p. 8).

☐   I have memorized five Scripture passages and recorded my progress on page 7.

# *Friday, Date* ☐

*Read Colossians 2:13–15.*

1.  Yesterday you read Jesus' prayer for his disciples as he anticipated his crucifixion. He prayed specifically that God would protect them from the evil one. Today's passage, written years after the crucifixion, declares Christ's triumph over the powers of evil. According to verses 13–14, what did his victory on the cross do for you personally?

_____

_____

2.  Notice the last phrase in verse 15: "He made a public spectacle of them, triumphing over them by the cross." In Roman times, victorious generals would return publicly with their vanquished enemies in a parade of triumph. Picture yourself watching a parade where your enemies are being led away. What words might describe your emotions?
    __ Liberation
    __ Celebration
    __ Gratitude

    __ _____
    __ _____

3.  In verse 14 Jesus is said to have nailed the Law with its regulations to the cross. With this graphic imagery in mind, reread verse 15. This is not just a ho-hum "God wins" verse but a passionate declaration of victory. How does Christ's triumph calm your fears of the rise of evil?

_____

_____

4.  Take a moment to thank God for making you alive in Christ and for triumphing over evil.

☐ I have prayed the Facing Down Our Fears Prayer today (see p. 8).

☐ I have memorized five Scripture passages and recorded my progress on page 7.

☐ I have been a Barnabas for three people and recorded my progress on page 10.

☐ I completed my outrageously courageous act and evaluated my effort on page 41.

# *Saturday, Date* ☐

*2 Thessalonians 3:3* ◄━ **Memory Verse Option**

1. This verse assures believers of protection from the evil one. The preceding chapter describes the man of lawlessness. Skim chapter 2. How does that impact the way you understand today's verse?

_____

_____

2. What two promises does Paul give in this verse? Have you seen those promises fulfilled in your life recently? If so, how?

_____

_____

3. List three fears you have regarding the rise of evil. How does this verse help calm your fears?

   1. _____

   2. _____

   3. _____

_____

_____

4. Notice Paul's final comments in 2 Thessalonians 3:16. For the last 50 days you've been praying about areas in your life where you're not at peace. What difference has that made?

_____

_____

5. What is a favorite hymn, chorus, or poem that reflects the faithfulness of God? (You might consider making up one of your own.) Sing or pray these words to God now.

_____

☐ I have prayed the Facing Down Our Fears Prayer today (see p. 8).

☐ I have memorized five Scripture passages and recorded my progress on page 7.

*Sunday, Date* ☐

*Read 1 Peter 1:3–5.*

1.   Make a list of the blessings this passage says have been given to us.

_____

_____

2.   According to verse 3, what makes these blessings available?

_____

3.   In verse 5 Peter writes that we are shielded by God's power through faith until Christ comes again. In what areas of your life are you especially thankful to know that God is shielding you from evil?

_____

_____

4.   Verse 6 says the blessings provided us through the resurrection of Christ give us reason to rejoice. How does the hope of our inheritance help you face down the fears of this life?

_____

_____

5.   Today is the last official day of our Adventure. What is one way you've grown in courage during this time? How can you carry this newfound courage into the days ahead?

_____

_____

☐   I have prayed the Facing Down Our Fears Prayer today (p. 8).

☐   I have memorized five Scripture passages and recorded my progress on page 7.

☐   I have filled out the Adventure comments form (see p. 79) and sent it to The Chapel of the Air.

**Don't miss the Follow-up Day on page 75.**

# ADVENTURING WITH FAMILY AND FRIENDS

**A**n adventure is always more exciting when you travel with someone else, and our 50-Day Spiritual Adventure is no exception! Here are some ideas to assist families and friends who want to work through the study together.

## Options for Adults

Many people find it extremely beneficial to have an accountability relationship with another adult who is participating in the Adventure. This might be a friend, a spouse, or another adult member of your family.

The simplest way to work with someone else is to complete the daily journal entries on your own, then occasionally meet together in person or over the phone to check on each other's progress.

Married couples, prayer partners, college roommates, and adult singles might choose a more in-depth approach. A daily or weekly fellowship time can be guided by discussing the questions for each day in the journal, or by using the questions in *How to Fear God Without Being Afraid of Him*.

Here are some other ideas you might use:

• Get together at the end of each week and talk about that week's topic and what you've learned. Take turns reading the related Scripture passages you've studied.

• Plan a get-together with other adult Christians to discuss the topic of fearing God. This will help you complete Discipline 5.

• Ask another Christian to listen to *The Chapel of the Air* radio broadcasts or the *How to Fear God Without Being Afraid of Him* audio book and discuss them with you.

• Invite a friend to join you in reading the book *Scared to Life* by Douglas Rumford. Discuss the reflection questions following each chapter.

## Journals for the Entire Family

As a help to families, we've created four different age-graded journals. They allow both adults and children to work through the same basic Adventure themes and assignments at the same time.

In addition to the Adult Journal, we have a Student Journal for junior and senior high schoolers, a Children's Journal for grades 3–6, and a Critter County Activity Book for children in kindergarten–grade 2.

Some parents like to go over the materials with their children on a daily basis. If you have younger children, this is actually a necessity. With this age-group, the Adventure activities often fit in nicely at breakfast or bedtime.

Older children may want to complete their journal after school so you can discuss what you're both learning over dinner.

Families with teens might want to schedule a weekly discussion over Friday night pizza. Some parents and teens work on their journals together. In most cases, however, parents will complete the Adult Journal on their own, then be available to help younger children with theirs.

Your family situation is unique. Feel free to adapt the Adventure to meet your family's needs.

## Adventure Themes (The Same, but Different)

During this Adventure adults will focus on eight fears we can "face down" with the help of a loving and powerful Father. These weekly themes have been adjusted to meet the special needs of each age-group.

**• Parents of Teens:** Except for Week 7, the themes for adults and youth are identical, though the Student Journal has been slanted to the specific needs of junior high and high school students.

Because the basic ideas and most Scripture assignments are the same, you can use this Adventure as an opportunity to get to know the spiritual side of your young adult. Ask for your son or daughter's opinion on the Scripture passages or for input on one of the questions in your journal. Teens may not feel comfortable sharing everything in their journal, but you can use the Adventure as an opportunity to open up discussion.

**• Parents of Children in Grades 3–6:** Your older grade school children can probably complete most of the journal entries and activities on their own. However, a child of this age enjoys the daily encouragement and affirmation of a parent. Complete your journal on your own, then use what you've discovered to add to what your child is learning. Work together on craft projects and Scripture memory.

**• Parents of Children in Kindergarten–Grade 2:** These little ones will need your active involvement to complete their journals. The Critter County Activity Book was designed as a "read to me" journal, helping children defeat the "Fearigators" that try to scare them.

After you've read the daily material together, have your child complete the activity provided. Then pray with your child, using the one- or two-sentence prayer provided for each day. This age-group has no disciplines to complete, but your child will be working on Scripture memory.

As a further help to families working together on the Adventure, here is a list of the eight weekly themes addressed in the Adult Journal along with changes we've made for children. You can refer to the information that follows in planning a daily or weekly Adventure family time.

As you work through these topics on your own, take time to talk to your child about what he or she is learning. Remember, one of the greatest things you can do for your children is to admit your own fears and be willing to talk about theirs. Note that one theme is addressed each week in the journal. The exception is Week 7, which deals with both themes 7 and 8.

**Week 1:** Face down the fear of a society that's breaking down. Older children will be learning about the fear of changes. Talk with them about losing a friend, changing schools, or getting braces. The Critter County Activity Book addresses common childhood fears such as the fear of animals, the dark, and storms. Share a story of something that scared you when you were young.

**Week 2:** Face down the fear of living insignificant lives. Children in grades 3–6 will be working on overcoming the fear of making bad decisions. Discuss the skills they are discovering for making good choices. Younger children can learn to make a difference by showing God's love to others. Help them think of some practical projects they can complete.

**Week 3:** Face down the fear of rejection. All ages will work on this same fear. Talk to your younger children about the fear of being laughed at. Ask older children about the fear of not being liked. Talk with teenagers about peer pressure.

**Week 4:** Face down the fear of the big "F" (failure). All ages will work on this same fear. Talk with teens and children about the fact that our value to God is not based on our achievements. Brainstorm biblical examples of people who risked failure to act on God's behalf.

**Week 5:** Face down the unhealthy fear of God. This is addressed in the book *How to Fear God Without Being Afraid of Him,* assigned reading for adults and students. Select some of the discussion questions from that book to open a sharing time with your teen. Older children will complete Trust Booster activities each day this week. These can be completed by the whole family as a discussion over lunch or dinner. Younger children will look at common lies about God told by Fearigators and learn a biblical truth to combat each of these lies. Discussing these lies is also a great family activity, because they are at the root of many adults' unhealthy fear of God.

**Week 6:** Face down the fear of sickness, aging, and death. This topic is addressed by all ages. Younger children will also talk about other events that cause sadness.

**Week 7:** Face down the fear of threats to our children. For teens, this topic will be broadened to address threats to their families. Older children will deal with the fear of danger. Younger children will take a practical look at ways to avoid danger by acting safely.

**Week 8:** Face down the fear of the rise of evil. Children will continue to look at dangers and how God can turn even bad situations into good. If you are completing this Adventure near Easter, talk with your children about how Christ conquered evil for all time when he rose from the dead.

## Tackling Disciplines Together

If you're a parent, take time to read through the introduction and discipline assignments in your child's journal. Younger children do not have disciplines, but related activities are sometimes suggested. Disciplines for teens are called Action Steps. For older children they are called Fear Busters. Although they have different names, many of the discipline activities are the same as yours.

**Everyone memorizes Scripture.** Adults will choose five of the eight Scripture passages listed in Discipline 1. Youth will memorize all eight of these same passages, one selection for each Sunday during the Adventure. Older children will memorize seven scriptures, one during each full week of the Adventure. These can be found inside the back cover of the Children's Journal. Younger children will memorize eight selections, one each Sunday. Both older and younger children have different memory passages from adults and youth, to accommodate their level of understanding.

**Everyone prays daily.** Adults and youth will both use the Facing Down Our Fears Prayer in Discipline 2. Older children will use the 9-1-1-G-O-D Prayer in Fear Buster 2. Younger children will use the short prayer written out at the bottom of each day's journal page.

**Everyone works on encouraging others.** Adults and youth will perform three encouraging acts during the Adventure. Older children will be writing three encouraging notes. You can help younger children give "love gifts" to others as described in Week 3 of the Critter County Activity Book.

**Everyone works on building courage.** Adults and youth will perform an outrageously courageous act. Older children will perform a Daring Deed for God. Younger children work to overcome the fear of trying new things.

**Everyone should keep on talking!** As a part of Discipline 5, adults and students are encouraged to get together to talk about how to cultivate a healthy fear of God. You can use the discussion questions in the book *How to Fear God Without Being Afraid of Him.* Older children complete their Fear Buster 5 by holding a "team meeting." For this assignment they need to interview an adult and a friend about their past and present fears using the questions on Day 36 of the Children's Journal. Younger children would also enjoy this activity.

# No Surprises Day 51

## FACING DOWN THE FEAR OF THE RISE OF EVIL

 **Pray**
Lord, show me how to bear up under difficult circumstances.

 **Read**
Peter's readers were going through hard times. We don't know exactly what their situation was, but we can learn a lot about coping with similar fears in our lives—including fear of the rise of evil.

**NOW READ: 1 PETER 4:12–19.**

 **Reflect**
Why have Christians suffered down through the centuries? What warning does Peter give?

**Don't let it take you by surprise** (12). Satan loves to catch us unprepared. For example, we might say to ourselves that because God loves us and is all-powerful, he would never let us suffer; but that only leaves us vulnerable to the enemy.

**Don't be content just to put up with it** (13). Sometimes Christians give the impression that as long as they don't actually give up under pressure, they are OK. But Peter calls us to do something much more positive—to rejoice in it. By the way we transform suffering we bring peace to ourselves, hope to others, and glory to God.

**Use it as material for praising God** (16). This is not the same as praising God for suffering or thanking him for the things—often evil things—which bring it. It is a determination to hang on to what we know to be true of God himself.

**Continue to fight the good fight** (19). Even in a world in pursuit of evil, we can persevere in doing good as we commit ourselves to God and faithfully serve him.

 **Apply**
"Do not be surprised..." (12). Peter's words are still a warning to us today. How are you facing down your fears and trials? How can you demonstrate to your family, friends, and society the reality of God (Matthew 5:15; 1Corinthians 15:58)?

 **Pray**
Lord, help me not to fear the rise of evil; give me such a full measure of your Spirit that I may be "more than a conqueror."

To order *Discovery* or other age-graded Scripture Union devotional resources see the order form on page 76.

Printed in the United States
R3389200001B/R33892PG201075BVX1B/1-15/A

9 781879 050471